Dare To Start

A Month of Devotions for Teen Guys

Frank Caudle

Chapter One

Stepping Out by Faith

Forget About the Jitters

*Give thanks in everything, for this is God's will for
you in Christ Jesus.*
1 Thessalonians 5:18 HCSB

Don't know how to pray or what to say? We've all been there and had those thoughts and questions. Where do we begin? Start with honesty. *God, I don't know what to say. I know you hear me. I want to thank you for another day. Could you help me to do better? Would you give me a Christian friend? One who will encourage me. Lord, I don't know much about the Bible, but I'm willing to learn. Would you help me? I'm willing.*

Prayer is talking—talking to God from the heart. It isn't a big deal. Just talk. He listens. Here's an interesting point that you may not know. God records all your prayers (Revelation 5:8). You know what? He likes to play them back. Why? They make Him happy. It's true. When someone genuinely cares, they listen to you. Sometimes we must vent, talk about it, and get it off our chest. You know what else? Our God is ready to listen.

We don't know everything; no one does. But holding it inside hurts us. Moses argued with God (Exodus 3 & 4). That's scary, but he did. God wanted Moses to talk to Pharaoh and tell him to release Israel from Egyptian bondage. Moses was scared. He said, "God, I can't speak right." God already knew that 1,000 years before. When God leads, he will do something. He will help you. Sure, there's nervousness, but you can do it. Just take the first step and then the second, then the next. Soon there's the realization. You're doing your impossible; this is when you realize with God's help, the impossible is possible. The only hurdle is us. Do you want to follow God's leading? If you do, that's your faith in action.

Forget about the jitters in your stomach. Instead, step forward, open your mouth and let God use you.

Something to think about.

- Have you ever felt intimated by the thought of praying? What did you do?

- When did you realize that praying is just talking to God? How did it change you?

- God has an instant replay button for your prayers. What do you think about that?

- Reading Exodus 3 & 4, we find Moses arguing with God. Have you ever argued with God? Who won and why?

- Moses told God, "I can't." Have you ever told God "I can't" and then did what He wanted you to do? What was the result?

- When did you do the "impossible" for God? How did you feel afterward?

Hurdling Personal Doubts

Do not be intimidated.
Jeremiah 1:17 CSB

There's something you can't stop thinking about because it keeps coming back. Right back where it started. We argue with ourselves. We even convince ourselves—no way I can do it. The mental weight keeps our shoulders bowed. Now, what? The pain won't leave. Maybe it's time to stop and ask, "God, is this you talking to me?" You may want to ask the Lord for confirmation. If your mind hears yes, then do it.

What God wants, he's willing and able to work all the circumstances out. Things will be ready when it's time, and the Lord will help you. That's his word. After doing whatever God requests, we'll see he was at work preparing everything and everyone in advance for the project he asked you to do.

The completion of his task brings relief. The result may even make us shake inside. Realizing that the God of the universe, the Father of our Savior, and the Holy Spirit used you is scary and thought-provoking. Yet the experience confirms that God is in the details of life.

Sure, we knew God used Bible personalities in the past, but that was then. Now it's personal, and he is using you. That's exciting.

You're part of his plan. Maybe the only person in the world who could do what you did. Now, that will knock your socks off! Later, thinking and then trembling, you realized God used you. He really used you. But that's just the introduction—he still wants to use you. Are you available again? If so, get ready. There's another opportunity ahead. A warning, though, don't get overconfident or proud. If you do, the Lord will humble you. That's a hard lesson to learn.

Hurdling personal doubts and trusting God can be hard at first, but with his help, nothing is impossible for him.

Something to think about.

- Are you easily intimated? If so, by whom and why?

- Ask the Lord your questions. He doesn't mind answering them. How did Jesus answer you? Explain.

- It's hard to step out by faith, but in hindsight, you see the Lord had everything ready. Write your journey of how the Lord provided.

- Explain some details that God connected for you to fulfill his instructions.

- Are you willing for God to use you again? If so, how are you better prepared to serve him?

- Personal doubts are part of life. Remember this, the Lord used you before, and he is anxious to use you again. Are you still willing for him to use you? Explain.

We Have a True Friend

When I kept things to myself, I felt weak deep inside me.
I moaned all day long.
Psalm 32:3 NCV

Everyone needs someone to talk to. Whether a friend or someone you respect, but someone who will be honest. Brutally honest if that is what you need. A homeboy who will keep his mouth shut. Someone trustworthy.

Usually, we don't share everything, even with the best of friends. Some things are private. Real private. Yet, there are times when we tell no one, not even God.

That's a mistake on our part. Why? Because Jesus already knows what's going on. Think for a minute; he already knows. The quicker we can grasp that thought, the better off we will be. Jesus is willing to help. But we need to ask. Without asking for his help, we'll lose. So, it seems like we should swallow our pride and stubbornness, ask for help, and get on with life.

The pride thing will make us suffer needlessly. Ask God for help. When we let our stupid arrogance get in the way, someone suffers. Guess who that will be?

Get alone somewhere, anywhere, and ask Jesus to help. Part of his ministry today is talking with his Father for us. When Jesus speaks to his Father, he listens.

I don't know about you, but I want all the help I can get.

We make a big mistake in keeping our hurts to ourselves and not sharing our heartaches with God. Here's another thought. The Holy Spirit is your comforter. As a Christian, the Holy Spirit lives inside of you. Not only does he comfort you, but he also prays for you.

To me, knowing that Jesus and the Holy Spirit are talking to our heavenly Father about our request is reassuring. That alone gives me a feeling of inner peace. We have a true friend in Jesus.

Something to think about.

- What depresses you? Would you consider talking about it to someone? If so, did you feel better afterwards? Elaborate.

- Have you ever thought Jesus knows what is going on inside of you? You can talk to him. Would you talk to him? Why or why not?

- How has your pride hindered you spiritually? If your write your thoughts, they can be a source of relief.

- Are you willing to talk to Jesus about your false pride? How would you do that?

- Have you experienced the Holy Spirit comforting you? Reflect on what he did.

- Does the realization of Jesus and the Holy Spirit talking to our heavenly Father for you help you? Elaborate.

The Better Choice

I have good plans for you, not plans to hurt you. I will
give you hope and a good future.
Jeremiah 29:11 NCV

We all have weaknesses. Yes, we do. Now think about some of your weaknesses—patience, math, or organizational skills—then propose to change them to equip you for your up-and-coming new talent. Don't sit and ponder the what ifs. Make a determined effort to overcome your deficiencies.

Consider your strengths but be willing to expand your talents. For example, if math is your strong point, you may be good at problem-solving and figuring out what works. On the other hand, drawing diagrams for assembly could be your area of expertise if art is your talent.

I know a man who was an academic dropout in school. He now owns a lucrative heating and air conditioning business. He is kind, always wanting to help people. His wife manages the office.

Our strength is our talent. Everyone has at least one skill. Let God develop and expand your ability. When he does, your service for the Lord will increase.

Ask the Lord to help you uncover your raw talent. Then stick with it. Only God knows where the roads of your life will travel. Life is all about hoping things will work out for us. God can do mighty things through those who trust him. The future will reveal those who do. The trusting ones will allow the Lord to do his part. As we do our part, he will do his part. He will lead, equip, and provide all the ingredients when the time is right.

One other thing. Give God credit for your success. Without his help, our lives would be a miserable mess. Everyone has weaknesses, and everyone has talent. Which one to dwell on is your personal decision. Who will you trust, yourself or God? Which do you think is the better choice?

Something to think about.

- Do you believe God has a good plan for you? Why or why not?

- Have you recognized some of your God-given talents? What are they?

- Do not let your disappointments define you. Give two reasons why. Explain each one.

- Do you believe God wants to use you? If your answer is no, Explain. Now look up Philippians 4:13. Is your answer still the same?

- New talent emerges when needed. Why is patience required here?

- Why is dwelling on past failures a lack of faith?

Chapter Two

Asking for Guidance

A Grandmother's Prayer

For I am mindful of the sincere faith within you, which first
dwelt in your grandmother Lois.
2 Timothy 1:5 NASB

She was an old lady, ancient to me. She could hardly walk or so I thought. What good was she? She was someone's grandmother. Such people should get out of the way; they're just occupying space—valuable space. They lived their lives—they should give their money to someone young who knows how to live—the ones who know how to enjoy life and have fun.

All grandmothers are old. She's the parent of your parents, but with all that experience, she knows a few things. So yes, she is wiser than any grandchild could ever dream.

Her name is Lois. She's a grandmother. She has a daughter; her name is Eunice. Their names appear only once in the Bible. That's important. God chose to record their names. Why? Because they prayed. Prayed for a young man named Timothy. He came to know the Lord because Lois knew how to pray. Not only pray but live a Godly life in front of Timothy. He will be one of the apostle Paul's best preachers. If you remember, Paul wrote two letters to him. They're in the Bible.

That didn't just happen. Lois, the saintly grandmother, started praying regularly for her grandson. She also asked God to use her daughter Eunice to raise her son, Timothy, correctly in spiritual matters.

You see, a grandmother's prayers have power, far-reaching power. They could be prayers said years before you were born, but God waited until the right time to answer them.

Timothy didn't know how many prayers granny prayed, but God did. A godly older woman knew how to pray. An everlasting God knew how and when to answer them.

If you wonder why, you keep thinking about spiritual things while you're trying to ignore them but can't, your wondering could be your grandma's prayers are being answered.

There is one thing for sure; you cannot outrun a grandmother's prayers. You can run but God will catch you. You can try to ignore those reoccurring thoughts, but you never will. Instead, you'll be miserable until you finally give in. So, let God answer your grandmother's prayers for you.

When you get to heaven, you and your grandmother can enjoy eternity better because of her prayers.

Something to think about.

- Have you ever tried to ignore that nagging thought about God? What happened?

- When your grandmother reminds you about church, what do you think? Why would they ask such a thing?

- What do you wish you knew about growing up in your grandparent's teen years?

- What would you ask your grandparent about their peer pressure?

- If Granny could change anything in you, what would it be and why?

- Would you take her advice? Why and why not?

No! Can Be Good

Therefore, brothers, be patient.
James 5:7 HCSB

God doesn't always answer your prayers immediately. You don't like it. And you can't understand why. The Bible states he hears our request, "I waited patiently for the LORD, and He turned to me and heard my cry for help" (Psalms 40:1). "A patient spirit is better than a proud spirit" (Ecclesiastes 7:8)

We reason within ourselves. If the Lord hears our requests, why doesn't he answer them? He replies I do answer your petitions. Just not the way or when you want. His methods, thoughts, and timing are better than ours. He knows what is best and when the time is right. We think we do. But Jesus sees the long-range results; he always chooses what is better. Tomorrow, next year, or ten years from now, may be his answer. He truly knows best, and we don't. We may think we do now, but later, we'll realize God knew what he was doing.

One thing we need to remember and remind ourselves, God doesn't explain himself as to when or why. That's where our faith comes into place—trusting him when we don't understand. I know it's hard to do. But faith says we can trust him to do what's best all the time.

When we rely on him, somehow, everything works out eventually. Then, we understand why Jesus waited to answer or why he chose not to grant our requests.

As you pray more, you grow spiritually. Receiving a definite no from God helps you to mature in mysterious spiritual ways.

Your parents have told you no many times. You didn't like their answer, but life went on. You survived. Later, you realize why they said what they said. Parents know more than we think, and so does our God.

Our wise parents knew their answer was for everybody's good, not just for you. The same principle applies to God's answer to your prayers.

Something to think about.

- Give three reasons why no can be good for you.

- List two reasons why God didn't answer your prayer immediately.

- Describe a patient spirit.

- Do your requests have long-range expectations? Why or why not?

- Try to explain your trust in God when you don't understand what he is doing in your life

- Do you find your faith grows as you pray more? Why or why not?

Not All Opportunities Are Right

We have small troubles for a while now, but they are helping
us gain an eternal glory that is much greater than the troubles.
2 Corinthians 4:17 NCV

When the situation doesn't make sense, what do you do? Do you follow the crowd or do what you think is the right thing? Is being with your peer group a greater priority to you than doing the right thing? Would you dare to be different?

If you read your Bible from cover to cover, you'll find unique individuals within its pages. They are different in places of birth and relationships. But they have something in common. Each is willing to be an individual—stand-alone people—even have a few trusted friends.

David, at one point in his life, had only one friend. A person he was willing to trust with his life. His name was Jonathan, King Saul's son. They made an unlikely pair.

At this point, David, who is part of the king's court, becomes Saul's thorn in the flesh. The citizens of Israel liked David more than their king. Saul didn't like it. As a result, Saul tried to kill David. First with a spear (I Samuel 19:10). Then he chased him all through Israel, but he couldn't catch him.

On one occasion, David was hiding in a cave. Saul wanted to take a nap in the same cave. After Saul was asleep, David tiptoed up to Saul, the villain, cut off part of Saul's garment, and then retreated deep into the cave. After Saul awakened and was on the other side of the valley, David called out the Saul. David, in the conversation, said, "I could have killed you. Here is proof holding up part of Saul's garment" (1 Samuel 24:10,11).

David had an excellent opportunity to carry out a dastardly deed but refused. Instead, David recognized God was in control because "All things work together for good to those who love God" (Romans 8:28 NKJV). David had the opportunity and the right to exact revenge, but he didn't. Instead, he believed God would work to resolve the situation for the good.

David trusted God to work the details out in the Lord's timing.

Life will throw us some opportunities to make a name for ourselves. But unfortunately, not all open doors are of the Lord. That's why you need to pray to ensure the Lord is opening the door. Satan is a counterfeiter. He can put an opportunity before you that looks good but will divert you from doing God's will. Not all opportunities are right for you. Remember that.

So, pray hard to enter the right door at the right time relying on God to work out the particulars.

Something to think about.

- Are you prone to follow the crowd? Why or why not?

- Can you stay true to yourself or surrender to peer pressure?

- When you can get revenge, what do you do?

- Are you willing to let God take care of the adverse situation, knowing his response is not an immediate one?

- Do you believe Romans 8:28 applies to you?

- Can you refuse to walk through an "open door" because you do not think God opened the door? State your reasons.

The Anxieties Disappear

I want you to be free from anxieties.
I Corinthians 7:32 ESV

Learning is difficult sometimes, especially when we don't like the subject.

There's a difference between your liking the subject and the subject liking you. Many feel that way about math; it doesn't add up. Others feel the same way concerning grammar. You think, "I can talk" and "why do I need to know about nouns, verbs, and adverbs?"

Whatever the dislikes, when test time comes, anxiousness is the feeling of the day. Many feel that way about God, yet there's a difference. Anybody can get to know the Lord if they are willing to put forth an effort?

One summer in high school, I decided to read my Bible. I opened it up to page one and started. It wasn't long before I got bogged down and quit. I didn't know that I should have started in the New Testament with the book of John, then First, Second, and Third John. Why these books? Because they're easier to understand. The other thing I wish I had known was to get a Bible translation I could understand.

Later, someone told me to pray before I started reading. Then, the Bible made sense to me.

So today, before beginning my devotion time, I pray. The Lord answers this prayer, giving me new insights into the things written in the Bible. First, he helped me to learn about him as I read the Bible. Then, between friends and church, my eyes started seeing what God wanted me to do.

One of the fantastic things that happened, I started praying a silent prayer before each meal and bedtime.

I know it's hard to pray in a noisy lunchroom when hundreds are talking. But that doesn't matter. Take ten seconds and say a silent prayer to thank the Lord for the meal. Sure, some stares will come, but there is a smile in heaven. Pleasing the Lord makes the anxieties disappear.

Try it and see what God will do.

Something to think about.

- Anxiety, suspense, and fear relate to uneasy feelings. Do any of these words describe your feeling about God? How would you express your thoughts concerning God?

- Have you ever started reading the Bible and quit? Why? Explain.

- Does praying before you start reading the Bible help?

- Has your devotion time helped you? Explain.

- How did your prayer life start, or do you need to start? Think this way—prayer is talking to God. So just start talking to him. (There is NO set pattern in what to say.) Write a summary of two of your prayers.

- Two months from now, revisit this devotion and write about your journey in prayer.

Never, Never, Ever

Be patient in time of trouble and never stop praying.
Romans 12:12 CEV

Trouble has a way of finding us at some of the most inopportune times. Satan knows all about our busy lives, especially when we don't have time for a hassle. The only way he can stop or slow us down is to throw up a roadblock of some sort.

So, what do we do? Quit or keep going for God. The Lord has a way of working things out for those who hang in there. Be patient and let God work. Did that sentence sink in? Patience is not something we want to hear or practice. Life has a way of helping us learn some of these lessons. When we don't understand, take a moment, and ask yourself, "What is God trying to teach me here?" "What do I need to learn?" Realizing this is your time to pray, then give God time to answer your prayer.

Prayer is your weapon. Satan can't stop your prayers from reaching God. The secret is to keep going for God; the Lord has a way of working things out. Be patient. Let God work. But in the meantime, pray some more. The devil doesn't like Christians praying, so he'll throw out all kinds of discouragements to make us doubt or try to get us to give up. But remember, he can't stop prayers. We can pray sitting in class, riding the bus, or walking to class. God is always ready to listen. Our Lord is always a prayer away, just a sincere prayer away.

One remarkable thing about trouble is that it can make us stronger Christians. Problems can be a nuisance. But, when we depend upon the Lord with patience, somehow God comes through. He solves the problem or gives us the grace to manage the situation because his answers develop our spiritual stamina.

God is good. He is with us when things are not going our way. Our Lord brings encouragement to us when times get challenging or emotional. He's always with us. Stop, look, and listen. He's there. His word is good. He will never, never, ever desert you. We are his children, and he loves us even when we don't function as we should.

Something to think about.

- Are you prone to make mistakes when you are in a hurry? If so, what do you need to change?

- Are you willing to let God work out the details or be partially satisfied with your own efforts?

- Remember, Satan cannot stop your prayers. Praying is a personal choice. What is your decision—pray or not pray? Defend your thoughts.

- Why doesn't the devil like for you to pray? Give three thoughts.

- Write about a time God didn't answer your prayer the way you wanted, but he gave you grace for the situation.

- Write about a time the Lord helped you in a tricky situation.

Chapter Three

Make Your Future Bright

Trophies Will Tarnish

Yet surely my just reward is with the LORD.
Isaiah 49:4 NKJV

Jazz's room is a trophy showcase. Everything he did, he was a winner. Most of us never win trophies.

What if we are not the best and don't win trophies? What are we to do? Never try. Give up. Give up on what? Games. School. What about life? Hope not. What's important? What we think is important now won't last. Sometime down the road something more exciting will appear.

Trophies will tarnish when stored in some box; you keep them and reflect upon the pleasant memories.

Life goes on. New quests for adventure are just beyond tomorrow. Experience tells us that everything here is temporary.

Make the experiences steppingstones through the streams of passing adversity. Leave the rocks in place for others to follow. Pave the way for fewer heartaches for others.

We're leaders when we arrive at this place in our life's journey. That thought may not enter your brain now. But others watch and learn from you. The spectators may be out of sight, but they are there.

Joseph's brothers (in the Bible) didn't know until years later that the young brat would save them from starvation. The thing is, Joseph kept going according to the Genesis account. Making the best of circumstances, he looked on the bright side of things. At times, his life didn't appear to be going anywhere except backward. Being faithful and dependable to God always pays off. Our problem may be the payoff doesn't come quick enough. But for the patient teen, everything works out in God's timing.

There may be no trophies in your room, but that can't stop you from encouraging others and yourself to keep going forward, trusting, and doing your best.

Something to think about.

- Are you a trophy winner? Does it matter to you? Explain.

- Have you found your niche? Elaborate.

- Are you learning from your experiences? If so, what are two of your lasting memories?

- Have you considered helping others? Or do you let them learn the hard way? What are your thoughts?

- Do you see yourself as a guide for others? What would it take for you to step out of the shadows?

- Are you willing to make some good memories? If so, how?

What's Your Dream?

But one thing I do: forgetting what is behind and
reaching forward to what is ahead.
Philippians 3:13 HCSB

The sun looks the same as it did yesterday. It's the same sun Adam saw thousands of years ago and will be the same sun that you will see tomorrow.

Some things don't change, but we do. Each new day has its adventures and challenges, even new learning experiences. School is one area of our learning process. Academics is one thing, but our social life is quite another. When friends are changing, life can be discouraging as well as encouraging. What do we want? For many of us, we just let life happen. We don't think about what's new to learn and experience. We let life come our way.

There's a new world out there, and everyone can experience it and open new doors. All it takes is a desire and a go-get-them attitude. Don't sell yourself short. If success is the goal, what's the plan? Most football teams do not score on every possession. Does that stop the team from its desire to score a touchdown? The repeated effort brings the score.

How badly do we want the dream? If it's our goal, discipline is required to accomplish our aspiration, but it can happen.

In the meantime, keep on plugging along in other areas, too. Entertain yourself, read new material, and go to unusual places and events. Finding the secret ingredient or procedure to the dream may be in the most unexpected place.

Sure, setbacks may appear, but all shortcomings say one thing, it wasn't the time or the place. Perseverance often pays whopping dividends.

What's your dream? My high school dream was architecture. I loved to design houses and buildings. But I had a head-on collision with calculus, and I lost! A change was necessary. Then, one day, my life's ambition changed. Sure, the journey has been challenging, but I like helping people. That's my true dream. What's yours?

Something to think about.

- Someone has asked you in the past, what do you want to do when you grow up? Have you changed your answer? What is your dream now?

- Do you have a relentless desire to achieve your goal? What are your plans to achieve it?

- Are you willing to learn more about how to achieve your desire? In what ways?

- Have you ever watched a hairstylist who can talk about anything? Their secret is their willingness to listen and expand their knowledge beyond hair. How will listening help your reach your dream?

- Achievers never quit. What makes you keep going towards your dream?

- What's your backup plan?

Our Adventure, Our Calling, Our Purpose

"Did God actually say?"
Genesis 3:1 ESV

Every state has an age requirement to receive a driver's license. Usually, the age is sixteen to eighteen, depending upon the state. Even the military has an age requirement for entrance. Also, some churches have pre-requisites (age or completion of training classes) to receive baptism and participation in communion.

Does God have age restrictions to experience forgiveness? I can't find an age written in the Bible. How young is too young to pray? Many parents teach their children to pray as soon as they can talk. Age is only a number. God looks beyond the years and examines the heart.

God calls young people to ministry. Joseph was seventeen (Genesis 37:2). Jeremiah said he was too young to be a prophet (Jeremiah 1:7). Whatever your age, God can use you.

Any time the Lord wants you, he'll speak directly to you. For many, Jesus confirms his calling in our teen years. His tender voice speaks to your heart. Then, he waits for you to respond. Reaching the moment of commitment can be difficult. Perhaps an inward struggle—one that will not go away. The only workable solution is the surrender of your will to him. When we accept God's calling, our adventure begins.

Don't panic if you have doubts. Ask God for confirmation. The Lord is willing to confirm his wishes for you. When he does, go ahead and follow his lead. He will gently guide you every step of the way. That's his promise. Now the devil will try to scare you from accepting God's invitation to serve the Lord Jesus. Satan will cause you to doubt. Please don't listen to him. When doubts come, that is a sure sign that God has something special for you to do.

Saying yes to God has no age requirement. But there is a heart requirement. Is your heart willing to let God be in control of your life?

If so, expect an adventure, a purpose, and the joy of knowing that you are a encouragement to others.

Something to think about.

- Which is more important to God—age or your heart? Defend your answer.

- When God speaks to your heart, how do you respond?

- Describe the first time you thought God was speaking or leading you.

- Did you understand, or did you wrestle with the Lord?

- God always keeps his word. Are you willing to trust him? Why?

- Is your heart ready to let God lead you on an adventure? If yes. Describe your anxieties.

Chapter Four

Following Directions

Your Best Interest

Whoever listens to me will live in safety.
Proverbs 1:33 NIV

Do I go, or do I stay? The question is simple, but the answer may not be. Whichever way the response goes, one may ask themselves, how do I know what God wants me to do?

God wants to be in our plans which means he desires to be in our decision-making. He prefers his children to do what he wishes. But the choice is ours and ours alone. Are we ready for his advice? One thing is for sure, the Lord knows best. We may think about why. The answer is he knows the future.

If we're serious about knowing what God wants us to do— ask. Take time to get alone, find a quiet place, and ask the Lord for his leadership. Then wait for him. He may give you a thought. One that you've never considered before. If so, you want to ask for confirmation if you are still unsure. God doesn't mind if you ask again. Gideon did, and God validated his request (Judges 6:37 ff). Then Gideon went on to accomplish God's will and won the victory.

Obedience is the goal of every Christian. Sometimes fear or doubts may hinder us. This insecurity is not unusual. It happens to every believer. Trusting God is hard sometimes, but the Lord works out the details.

We may not understand the outcome, but obedience gives us peace of mind. Being compliant with God surpasses understanding.

When your parents or an authority figure warns you by saying no to you, their warning is for your benefit. But no one likes to hear the word no. Typically, good advice goes unappreciated at the time.

When God tells you no, he is looking out for your best interest. Your conscience will lead you and confirm his answer if you listen. Will you do that?

Something to think about.

- How have following instructions helped you?

- Has God influenced your decision-making? Explain.

- If Gideon can ask repeatedly for God's answer, so can you. Are you willing to wait for his answer? Explain how God answered your request.

- How does obedience work in your favor? Give two examples.

- Explain the calm feeling after you have made the right decision.

- Does the inner peace confirm your relationship with God? Why?

Satisfaction Is Personal

So if we have enough food and clothing, let us be content.
I Timothy 6:8 NLT

Status is king in our world. The more we have, the better off we are. Is that true? Do our possessions measure who we are? Everything our parents provided for us did not cost us a dime. Do clothes compute our inner worth? What about the shoes on our feet? Just because they are a particular brand, are we better than our classmates? If self-made values are possessions, what are we worth? Does God put a price tag on our souls?

God's tape measure goes around the heart. It doesn't measure your height or physique, but the spirit of your inner being, and the acceptance of others doesn't matter. Our relationship with Jesus is the most crucial thing in our lives. He is the one who paid our sin debt and eradicated the sins of every Christian. Only the Lord's shed blood could pay that sum!

We usually don't compare earthly importance to heavenly worth, but what does our heavenly Father see when he looks at us? Stylish clothes of a sinner or the blood-washed clothes of a saint.

What satisfies—looking good or a peaceful night's sleep? Satisfaction has two definitions: one, the fulfilling of our needs or pleasures. Two, the fulfillment of our wrongs made right. In other words, is the penalty of my sin taken care of?

Contentment, according to our verse, has two thoughts. First, they are food and clothing. If there is a meal before you, be satisfied, even if it's spinach and brussels sprouts or eggplant. Are the clothes on your back clean? Are they old hand-me-downs or new? Whatever they are, be satisfied. More than a million other teens in the world don't have the possessions you have.

Your heart matters more to God than anything else!

Something to think about.

- Do your possessions best measure your self-worth? Explain.

- Besides academics, what is your focus? Could you elaborate?

- Can your present social and spiritual life coexist? Are they in harmony? Why or why not?

- Which do you prefer—fulfillment or forgiveness? Why?

- What is your definition of contentment?

- Have you changed your definition of satisfaction? If so, how?

Look At the Heart

Be fair in your judging. You must not show special
favor to poor people or great people, but be fair when
you judge your neighbor.
Leviticus 19:15 NCV

What makes us choose one person over another? Looks, influence, is it always about what we can get? We make choices in pickup games of football and basketball. We choose the better-skilled person before the unskilled.

How do you decide which girls to talk to? The good-looking ones or the less attractive ones? Even in church, we practice the same pattern. What about the spiritual young lady is she your first choice? What is your criteria for your decision?

Actions reveal our thoughts. Often selfish thoughts. Our footsteps speak louder than our words.

When your youth director or pastor speaks about choices, are you listening, is your mind wandering, or saying no way? Whatever the decision, you made it. All your instructors made their mistakes, many of which they regret. They want you to learn not to make the same mistakes. The question is, are we willing to listen?

Hopefully, we'll listen and apply their lessons to our lives. Then we'll not have the same regrets as they do.

What we tend to do is judge everything by looks. As a result, our first impression is often wrong. Our appearance has to do with genes, which no one controls. However, the inner appearance is what we make. Our character exhibits our authenticity. The real person. The true individual. The part that hopefully will improve. The person who is genuine somehow always improves.

We need to look beyond the outward appearance and look at an individual's heart.

Character always trumps beauty.

Something to think about.

- Are we fair in our decisions? Defend yourself.

- Should all our choices be for our interests, or should we consider others? Why?

- What are some of your actions that spoke louder than your words? Any regrets? If so, name two.

- Have you ever made a mistake and regretted it? Was it a big one? If you could, how would you change it?

- Do your friends see you the way you want to be known?

- Have you sensed that integrity speaks loudly? If so, in what way?

Life Is Not Fair

God treats us much better than we deserve.
Romans 3:24 CEV

Life is so unfair. How did this happen to me, you may ask? I don't understand. I didn't do anything wrong or illegal.

Everyone thinks these thoughts at times. It just depends on the day. But just because things don't go our way—doesn't mean God or anybody else is punishing us. Life happens to the good and the bad, including things we don't understand. It's just the way some things are.

There are a lot of things to be thankful for. I have ten fingers and toes, a roof over my head, and plenty to eat. That's more stuff than billions of others have on this earth.

I'm thankful for my birthplace; I could have been born to a tribe in the Amazon.

My Dad had a job and provided us with a place to live. It wasn't a mansion but a rental house which was not in the greatest of areas.

Life was good. I had health, food, and clothing. Whatever our situation, we need to be grateful.

Then there is another thing about life—the inner joy that God gives us. Stop and think about who supplies the provisions at home. Who paid for them? Do we deserve them? Do we need all we have? What makes us so privileged as compared to the rest of the world?

No, life is not fair, but it could be worse. Stop complaining. Give thanks. If you're still selfish after reading this, why don't you have a long talk with God? Ask him how to change and be thankful for what you have.

Something to think about.

- Does God treat you better than you deserve? Explain.

- Do you believe bad things happen to good people? Defend your thoughts. Give three examples.

- What do you think when you look in the refrigerator and don't see what you want? Before you answer—remember over half of the world's population does not have a fridge.

- Are you grateful for what you do have? Why?

- Why are you special in God's eyes? Explain.

- Will complaining advance your position in life? List some of your complaints. What can you do to turn things around?

Chapter Five

Focus – Staying on Track

An Acceptable Applicant

He trusted me and gave me this work of serving him.
I Timothy 1:12 NCV

Every believer is a doorkeeper. We stand there either in the way of someone or to open the door for them. Do you ever open a door for someone? Did they say thank you? Most people under the age of twenty-five don't. Don't believe me, try it.

It's one thing to open a physical door. It's better to open a spiritual door for another.

We are the best door opener or gatekeeper our friends will ever know. Why? They know us. Trust us. They've seen how we operate. They know if we're a phony or the real deal.

Our reputation precedes us. If we're a person who others can rely on, they will trust us. Trust our words and actions.

At our age, we don't think about character building. We may not even consider it.

When filling out our college application, what matters? What is a deal-breaker among equally qualified applicants? The university is looking for extracurricular activities. Are we social? Can you write an interesting essay? Do we belong to service organizations? Perhaps hold an office in them. Those are door openers.

Yes, grades are important. However, many times, they are only the foundation for consideration. Survival in the college scene includes your study habits and using your time wisely. If we have a history of good grades and can manage our time to do other things, we'll be considered the better applicant.

Life is about managing our responsibilities well and putting our Bible into practice.

I Timothy 1:12 states this principle powerfully, "I thank Christ Jesus our Lord, who gave me strength, because he trusted me and gave me this work of serving him" (NCV).

Our challenge is to do well so our lives will be better.

Something to think about.

- Do other adults consider you polite or rude? Why?

- What are some of your mannerisms that need improving?

- Do you care what others think or know about you? Why.

- Are your responsibilities paving the way to a brighter future?

- What Bible principles are you practicing now? Are they preparing you for a better future?

- Will your lifestyle practices now bring regret later?

Make A Sign

May integrity and uprightness keep me, for I wait for You.
Psalm 25:21 HCSB

Right is always right. You've heard those words before, but are they true? Who knows what is right? Well, there's good news. Everyone has a conscience—our directional compass to life's decisions.

When anyone does anything wrong, something inside them starts the flashing warning lights. Or maybe it's a sound system with a weird alarm. So, when we hear this alarming sound inside us, we need to back off. Way off.

Following rules at home or school isn't always welcoming in our thinking. Rules are guidelines in place because of someone's wrongdoing. A wrong decision or stubbornness was usually the root cause. Disobedience can be as simple as refusing to read labels. Printed labels are beneficial. When a bottle has the big red word poison, the contents are dangerous. Most work vehicles and heavy equipment make a warning sound when backing up. The sound warns people to get out of the way because the driver can't see directly behind the vehicle.

Our conscience is our warning light saying something isn't right. So, when our conscience kicks in, look up. God's warning system is going off. To ignore it means trouble. Sometimes big trouble. All spiritual problems have one thing in common: missing the warning. Every sin has a price, many of which are long-lasting—a lifetime for some.

When we play with sinful fire, we get burned. The scars and memories never go away.

Uprightness, doing the right thing, keeps the individual safe in the eyes of the Lord. Peers may disagree, but that's their choice. Correct decisions will have eternal rewards.

Make yourself a sign and post it in a prominent place for important upcoming decisions. For example, by the light switch in your bedroom, the Post-it Note should include, "What is best for eternity?

Doing the right thing is always worthwhile in the end.

Something to think about.

- Does your conscience ever bother you? How do you react?

- When your conscience sounds its warning, how do you respond? Explain.

- Are rules in place because they are stupid or to help you? Elaborate on one.

- Has God ever sounded the warning alarm for you? What did you do? Did you make a good decision?

- Have you ever been burned by sinful fire? What was the lesson for you?

- Have you ever asked yourself, "What is best for eternity?" What were the immediate results?

Everything Is Connected

My son, pay attention to my wisdom, listen
well to my words of insight.
Proverbs 5:1 NIV

Do we like to hear advice from someone old? Probably not. Our reasoning is that they're old; we think, how could they understand what's going on in my life? That is true, but we don't realize our parents and grandparents have experienced life for years. Not the same events, but similar situations give them experience and great insights that you don't have.

Every situation is a repeat of another past episode of life. It's true because man's nature is still the same. Temptations are everywhere, and human reasoning doesn't change. Happiness is happiness, and greed is still the same old greed. Every day still has 24 hours. Teen years are still the same. Clothing and gadgets in technology have changed, but human nature hasn't changed.

We all want to learn about new things, but are these gadgets suitable for us? It's our choice.

Choices originated in the Garden of Eden. Unfortunately, Adam chose to listen to the wrong advice. Adam decided he wanted to taste another fruit, the forbidden one.

His decision cost him dearly. His sin impacted succeeding generations, including ours. That's scary when you think about it. Everything we do affects others.

We can't see the future, but everything we do or don't do has long-range effects, even how homework affects our grades. Grades can determine one's additional training. The college or our apprenticeship determines the amount of money we make, which determines the car we purchase. Our income limits the size of our house and where we live.

See, everything is connected. Listening in class has long-range effects. Following the advice of the Lord causes our days and tomorrows to be brighter.

We need someone to show us the next step. Are we willing to let someone help us?

Something to think about.

- Do you respond well to advice? Why or why not?

- Do you believe history is in a repeating cycle? How does that affect you? Are you willing to learn from others?

- Situations may change, but life principles remain the same. Are you willing to learn principles—why or why not?

- Would you rather learn from others or make your own mistakes?

- Do you believe doing or neglecting homework has long-range effects?

- Are you willing to ask for help? Why or why not?

Your Earning Potential

I will guide you along the best pathway for your life. I will advise you and watch over you.
Psalms 32:8 NLT

Every day, in every class, someone tries to put more information into your head. Are there any more gigabytes of memory left, you may ask? After all, there's a life out there after school.

The truth is life is all about learning and applying things we've learned. The information we receive increases our potential for future accomplishments. Every layer of knowledge strengthens our life's journey.

I know you're wondering, "Why do I need this?"

The answer may be elusive now, but rest assured the information will come in handy sometime in your future. For example, when completing an employment application. An algebra question could be the qualifying question on an entrance test for a job. So could learning how to read a ruler or tape measure. Adding and subtracting correctly will ensure the company's bank deposit is correct. If these skills are deficient, the employer may face unwanted financial embarrassment and penalties. Later, when acquiring a personal credit card, pay attention to the interest rates and the stated credit limit. Again, credit card companies take advantage of poor math skills and the failure to read the fine print.

Life doesn't come with a tour guide beyond your parents. Soon you will be a number lost in the sea of humanity.

Here's a piece of advice you may not want. Do your best in school and learn all you can in every class. Why? Your earning potential hangs in the balance.

Something to think about.

- Do you feel like some of your classes are useless? Explain.

- Do you or do you not believe your classes will benefit you later? Why or why not?

- Why is a broad base of knowledge beneficial? Write your thoughts.

- What qualities do you have that say you are special?

- How do you accept advice from older people?

- Give your thoughts on why your future stands on your accomplishments now.

No Guilt

Doing what is right and fair is more important to the Lord.
Proverbs 21:3 NCV

One's conscience can speak loud and clear as if God is using a bull horn. Our minds can deceive us. The mind doesn't work as a math problem with only one answer. Instead, our brain likes choices. Sort of like a multiple-choice test, but there is only one correct answer, and the rest are incorrect. If you're guessing, chances are your answer will be wrong. One out of four or five isn't good odds. You have a 75 to 80% chance of being incorrect.

Life can be a big multiple-choice test. Meaning, that without knowing God's Word (His only guidebook), chances are not suitable for making the correct choice.

Having the inside track to know and do right is an advantage. Our relationship with God triggers the conscience to decide what is best. If we wrestle with God, that's a losing situation. Obedience may sound easy for some, but for many of us, it's not. Why? We try to analyze everything. We tend to be looking for pleasure in the answer. Sure, wrong decisions in life may seem pleasurable, that is for a while. But short-lived happiness with long-range consequences is a bad exchange. Wanting what is best in our lives is always the desired choice.

A peaceful conscience is one of the good things about making the right choice. AKA, your heart. There's no guilt associated with the correct choice. Instead, the simple by-product (science lesson in action) is an inward peace that provides a clear conscience.

God is in charge. He can even apply school subjects to everyday decision-making. That's amazing when you stop and think about it.

Something to think about.

- Is being right and fair before the Lord important? Defend your thoughts.

- Is it better to live by God's rules? Why or why not?

- If you wrestle with God, what are your chances of winning?

- Are you willing to wait a while for true happiness, or do you want temporary joy with regrets later? Which is better for you? Explain.

- Is having a clear conscience meaningful to you? Why or why not?

- Do you allow God to be in charge of your life? If so, are there any benefits? Explain.

Chapter Six

Parting Ways

Place Of Discord

He stirs up trouble.
Proverbs 6:14 CSB

I looked out my window; of all things, there was this dandelion. It stood out beyond the trees and kids playing in the yard. So, why comment on such a thing?

What can I learn from a dandelion? What an odd question.

These pesty plants and some classmates have much in common. Like weeds, they show up where they are not wanted. These individuals have a way of being noticed. Not in a good way, but there they are—the strange ones in the crowd.

Their mannerisms and clothing are different, accenting their non-verbal communication. They're not like the rest of us.

This dandelion was taller than the grass, grabbing my attention. Yet, it was still in its youth. How do I know this because its brisk hairs were swaying in the breeze? Then, springing back to its original posture as the wind died down. The brittle flower could sense the anticipation for the next gust of wind. This dandelion enjoyed each sudden gust of wind, as only youth can do. As the days passed, its stem became stiffer, and its hair started to turn loose.

Soon, the seeds of discourse began to disperse: one here, another one there. You could sense something ugly was going to happen.

Then the evitable happened. It was a kick. Intentional, by someone, of course. But the stem snapped, and its brisk hairs shot forth in every direction.

The seeds of discouragement were going everywhere. They soon disappeared, never to be retrieved. They were blending into their surroundings, seemingly unnoticed. They were quiet, too quiet, and they even laid low for a while.

Then overnight, up pops the spring of trouble. Then another and another. Within a short time, the green grass of tranquility had its offshoots of troubling dandelions. They were everywhere—sowing irksome seeds of trouble.

Does your close-knit group have a dandelion starting to grow? If it does, unfortunately, their attention is growing faster than the rest.

Can you see the real intention? Are they peaceful, or are they planning to steal your friend?

All it takes is one lone dandelion to infiltrate the best yards in life. Then the yard whose pleasant and peaceful past becomes the place of discord. If there's a dandelion of discontentment in your circle of friends, trim it before it spreads or find a new circle of friends.

Something to think about.

- What does it take to get your attention? Describe two.

- How do you treat someone you do not want around?

- Why do you feel that way?

- Are you willing to get to know someone different? Why or why not? Explain.

- When you see a classmate negatively influencing a friend, what do you do and why?

- Can you walk away from a demoralizing situation? Explain.

No Regrets

*Oh, my lord, do not punish us for a sin that we have
so foolishly committed.*
Numbers 12:11 NRSV

Everyone experiences temptation, like taking an extra piece of cake. Then feeling uncomfortable afterward. It's too easy to say yes. Cheating on a test is easy. Social compromise gives way to peer acceptance in some circles. Everyone is dishonest at times, we say, so what's the big deal? Human reasoning can justify any action. If we want to participate in sin, we can find some way to make the situation right in our minds, at least for a while.

We want to say no. We know we should say no. Unfortunately, that three-letter word *but* causes people to stumble, fail, and often without recovery.

It's not okay just because others think so. Does your phone alarm get your attention? Sure, it does. Our conscience is our warning system. God is trying to get your attention. Saying don't do it!

We should listen when we hear the Lord's voice speaking to our conscience. No one else in the room will sense what you hear. Why? Because conviction is personal, out of your control. God is trying to get you to listen, and you can't turn the volume down. The Lord is reminding you; that you have the power to say no to sin.

If you want peace of mind ten minutes or ten months from now, say no. Do you want your parents to know what you're doing? You may say, "no way will they ever know." You're mistaken. They always find out sooner or later; someone always talks. The revealing time will be embarrassing, maybe with long-range effects, which you don't want to have.

If we want to say no to sin, then say it and do it. God promises to help us. He will not let us down if we ask. We should realize he is always with us and gives us the strength to continue. Then, we can sleep well at night with no regrets.

Something to think about.

- Have you noticed you can justify your wrongs? Does your reasoning make it right? Explain your answer.

- Does the word *but* get you in trouble? Defend your reasoning.

- Are you glad conviction is personal? Would you want others to know your sins? Explain your thought or thoughts.

- If you don't want your parents to know, should you allow yourself to do what you are considering? Write a paragraph to explain.

- Have you had an embarrassing past event revealed to a new girlfriend? How did it make you feel?

- Has claiming one of God's promises been advantageous for you? Explain.

Letting Go

Give all your worries to him, because he cares about you.
I Peter 5:7 NCV

Trying to help someone who doesn't want your help is discouraging. You may throw up your hands and think, go ahead, fall on your face. But don't ask me to help you get up.

Turning down help is limiting yourself. As a result, you'll be underachieving your potential. Everyone needs help at times. Being stubborn only hurts you and delays your progress in life.

Today is another opportunity to succeed. To do so requires focus. For the Christian, it means asking for the Lord's guidance and making yourself available to him. Then allow God to work through you by doing whatever he wants you to do.

I know you want to do it yourself. We always do. That's the pride in us. We want to prove something to someone, maybe even to ourselves. Do you think looking to God is a weakness? To some, it sounds stupid. But be dumb enough to lean on God for strength and guidance. Even praying before taking a test. Take ten seconds and ask God to help you recall what you studied and the classroom lectures.

Many of your worries or anxieties will vanish once you write your name on the paper and answer the first question. If you find a question you don't know the answer to, skip it. Instead, answer everything you know, then go back and reexamine the unanswered questions. As you stare at the blanks, the answers may pop into your brain. If it doesn't, stop and pray again. The answer may come. It was like God said, "Okay, I'll help you because you asked. Now that you are depending on me and not yourself."

Those words may seem crazy. But try it. It's incredible how many times God answers those prayers.

Usually, the answers come. If not, you may even pray again. It's spot on how God answers. When you realize you don't know an answer? Write down something. Now and then, it's the correct answer. It's strange how God works.

One warning, don't expect God to bail you out of a situation when you didn't study. Our Lord does not bless laziness. He rewards diligence.

Something to think about.

- Is turning down help a good thing or a bad thing? Why?

- Are you ready for God to help you? If not, why? If so, why?

- How has pride affected your decisions? Was that a good or a bad choice? Defend your decision.

- Is this true? Once you start, good things begin to happen. Do you agree or disagree?

- Is reviewing your answers beneficial? Why?

- Why doesn't God bail you out of every problem? List three thoughts.

Knowing When to Say No

Do not go on presenting the members of your body to sin as
instruments of unrighteousness.
Romans 6:13 NASB

Failure is not a new phenomenon; it is as old as man. Failure goes back to Adam and Eve. It is all about temptation and the act of disobeying God. The disciples, Peter, James, and John, disobeyed Jesus in the Garden of Gethsemane. Jesus told them to pray. They didn't. They slept.

We make inferior grades because we do not study until we know the material. It's a choice we make. We let something else become a better priority in our minds.

Whatever diverts our attention is the temptation. It could be recreation, leisure, or entertainment, and it doesn't make any difference. It is some form of craving—a desire to be satisfied.

The essence of our problem is our wants. What do we want, pleasure, or the task before us? That decision process will follow you all your life. It started when you were very young and will follow you until your last breath unless you change.

No is a word we tell others. Do we ever tell ourselves no? No to an extra scoop of ice cream. No to getting up on time. No to the sin of temptation. No can save us a lot of grief.

The failure to heed the word *no* usually has adverse circumstances. For example, saying no to a speed limit sign can cost hundreds of dollars in fines and rising insurance premiums.

Saying no to your teacher can have adverse effects. Telling God, no for your desire to sin costs you big time in your relationship with him.

A warning thought before you use the word no, think about the consequences. Will using the two-letter word pay positive dividends or negative ones for you?

Something to think about.

- How do you choose your priorities? How would you change your decision-making process?

- Give two examples when you said yes instead of saying no.

- How are you better prepared to say no? Explain.

- Give three instances when you told yourself no.

- Give the results of ignoring your conscience.

- Have you told God no? What were the results?

Chapter Seven

Patience, I Need It

Big Dreams

God will generously provide all you need.
2 Corinthians 9:8 NLT

Some people have big plans. Others give up before their dreams come to fruition. Joseph, in the Bible, dreamed real dreams. He envisioned his parents and brothers would one day bow down to him. Joseph didn't know it would be years before it happened. But it did.

Joseph did not set out to be a big-shot power figure. But, through the leadership of God in adverse circumstances, Joseph became prominent. While in prison for a crime he didn't commit, Joseph interpreted some dreams for fellow prisoners. And his interpretations came true. Because he could discern the will of God in helping others, he eventually received a big promotion from prisoner to Prime Minister of Egypt in one day.

The apostle Paul, the missionary, also realized he could do remarkable things by depending upon God. So, he was bold enough to write, "God will generously provide" (2 Corinthians 9:6) and "I can" do all things through Christ (Philippians 4:13).

The teen years are not too early to ask God for his leadership in your life. But if you do and are persistent until he answers—the Lord will give directions. The Lord's leadership will be one step at a time process toward his ultimate goal.

Confidence in God's leading will lead to a lifelong adventure of trust. However, the trip will not be a road without potholes, bruises, and disappointments.

All journeys have them. Realize anywhere God leads, the devil will insert difficulties. Satan and faithless people will try to discourage you. Both Joseph and Paul were mistreated and jailed.

But they did not quit on God. They remained faithful, and more importantly, God used them during their trials. Their lives would have been incomplete if they stopped when the going got tough.

Remember, God does not change his mind often. Prayer is why the Lord will reconsider changing schedules or routes but not the destination (2 Kings 20:1-6). Why? Because he wants to use you for his glory.

Something to think about.

- What are your dreams? What would it take for you to make them happen?

- If the road to your dream gets hard, what will you do?

- Have you realized nothing is impossible with God? Explain.

- What are you willing to commit your life to in order to reach your dream?

- Are you ready to stay the course for the fulfillment if the road is long?

- What happens when the road gets bumpy? Remember, God doesn't change his mind.

Wait On the Lord

Those who wait on the LORD shall renew their strength.
Isaiah 40:31 NKJV

A loner has few, if any, friends. As Christians, we're never alone. The Holy Spirit lives inside of us. It's hard to comprehend, but it's true. We may have a problem realizing it at times. When we look at issues and situations, we also forget about Jesus. As a result, we feel alone and overwhelmed.

Sometimes we don't think about God helping us. That's our mistake—he's always ready to help. Of course, that doesn't mean the Lord bails us out of all our troubles. However, it does mean he is with us in our worst situations, protecting, comforting, and guiding us. If you're like me, you may expect everything to turn out great. But unfortunately, God doesn't work like that all the time.

There are great lifelong lessons to learn when things go in the wrong direction. Our bad decisions will help us never to make the same mistake again. The experience of a wrong decision is God's lesson for us to remember. We'll never forget it. How else will we learn? The lasting memories often come from our mistakes and errors. Hopefully, we aren't dumb enough to make them again (notice I repeated this thought for emphasis). Those are the ones we can share with others later if we dare.

When you think you're alone with no one to talk to, look up. God is ready to listen, help, and comfort you.

Comfort comes when you sit still and wait. Wait for God to give a thought or nudge in what to do for him.

Are you willing to wait and listen? Be still. Take notice of the quietness and stay with the Lord. Then you can hear his whispering voice.

Something to think about.

- Are you patient? What would it take for you to be unruffled?

- Does the thought of the Holy Spirit living inside you scare you or comfort you? Elaborate.

- Write down an example of God helping you.

- Write about a harsh spiritual lesson you experienced.

- How did the above event help you grow spiritually?

- Are you willing to wait on the Lord? Explain how waiting or not waiting helps you.

Do We Get the Picture?

Don't say, "I'll pay you back for the wrong you did." Wait for
the LORD, and he will make things right."
Proverbs 20:22 NCV

Holding a grudge isn't good. Did someone treat you wrong? What are you going to do about it? If getting even becomes an obsession, you lose. How can that be possible? I got even, and they got what they deserved.

Question. Who appointed you judge and jury? Did God? I don't think so. That's his responsibility.

Below are some scriptures emphasizing God's responsibility to do justice, not us.

Don't say, "I'll get even; I'll do to him what he did to me." (Proverbs 24:29).

"If someone does wrong to you, do not pay him back by doing wrong to him." (Romans 12:17).

Are you convinced yet? Let God do his work. He can do it better than you.

My friends, do not try to punish others when they wrong you, but wait for God to punish them with his anger. It is written: "I will punish those who do wrong; I will repay them," says the Lord. (Romans 12:19).

We know that God said, "I will punish those who do wrong; I will repay them." And he also said, "The Lord will judge his people." (Hebrews 10:30).

Let's turn the negative into the positive.

Wish good for those who harm you; wish them well and do not curse them (Romans 12:14).

But I say to you, love your enemies. Pray for those who hurt you. (Matthew 5:44).

Be sure that no one pays back wrong for wrong, but always try to do what is good for each other and for all people. (I Thessalonians 5:15).

Do we get the picture? Do good to those who mistreat you and let God take care of righting the wrongs.

Something to think about.

- Have you noticed a grudge hurts you? What can you do to remove your hurt?

- Is revenge the best long-term solution? Why or why not?

- Are you ready to let God take care of the situation? Are you willing to wait?

- How can you be nice to someone who hurts you? How would you do that? Give two examples.

- Praying for your enemies is hard—list three things you would ask God to help you pray for an adversary.

- List three ways other people would respond if you were friendly to the hurtful one.

There's Nothing New

There is nothing new under the sun
Ecclesiastes 1:9 NRSV

September means a new school year. January means a new calendar year, and tomorrow is a new day for you. But the rest of today is still an unknown. What does it hold? Will next week be different or just like all the rest?

Every day is a new opportunity. So, what will you do differently today? Trying out for a new sport may be on the schedule. Maybe applying for a learner's permit. How about praying in public for the first time? Whenever an opportunity arises is a chance to go into uncharted territory.

Years ago, going into space was thought to be impossible, but it wasn't. Man's been traveling to heaven for millenniums; that's space travel, and Lazarus did it and returned.

Deep-sea diving is not new. Jonah accomplished that feat years ago and didn't use scuba gear; he used a whale.

What about writing a book? Moses, David, Daniel, Matthew, John, and Paul wrote books. Thousands of years ago. Their books are in the Bible.

Joshua and Caleb are the only two men over sixty years of age to walk through two bodies of water on dry ground, the Red Sea, and the Jordan River.

"What has been is what will be, and what has been done is what will be done; there is nothing new under the sun" (Ecclesiastes 1:9 NRSV).

Because there is nothing new under the sun means somebody was there before you. Now it's your turn to try it. Just make safety a priority. New can be good for you, like learning to drive a car.

McDonald's is always hiring young people. Your school may even have a teacher cadet program which is a terrific way to see if you want to become a teacher.

Whatever the Lord allows, find a way to thank him for the opportunity and the chance to serve him.

Something to think about.

- Do you look forward to the future? Why would it be better?

- What's your dream? Write about it for a minute.

- Are you planning to accomplish your dream? How are you preparing?

- How is your dream like someone in the past?

- Why is learning something new good for you? Give two positive reasons as well as two negative ones.

- Why should you be thankful for a terrible experience? Explain.

Chapter Eight

Making Sure

Not Sure

Therefore, to him who knows to do good and
does not do it, to him it is sin.
James 4:17 NKJV

A mustard seed is a tiny seed about the size of a pinhead. Yet it can grow a tree that is about twenty feet tall?

When the mustard seed opens, the raw mustard is released. So, by adding vinegar and other ingredients, we get a tangy-tasting condiment to add to our food.

Why did Christ use the example of a mustard seed? To help us realize what faith can do. A tiny bit of faith can change people—faith also has a way of changing our behavior and attitudes.

Why is faith important? It is the foundation of all our rewards in heaven. Secondly, God states in the book of James, "If you don't do what you know is right, you have sinned" (4:17 CEV).

How does that apply to me?

Do right.

When?

All the time.

That's important. But we don't. The truth is we can't. We may not be guilty of shooting someone, but we could injure our friend with our words.

Okay, I can't do this faith thing all the time, we may say to ourselves. I know it's impossible. But that's the reason we're sinners in the eyes of God. For that reason, Jesus left heaven, came to earth, and died for humanity. When Jesus was on the cross, the daylight turned into the night for three hours. That's when our sins were on him. Yes, all the sins of everyone were on him. It was a terrible sight. His heavenly Father could not even look at his Son with all our sin. But it also proves just how much Jesus would do for us so we could go to heaven.

Not sure heaven is going to be your eternal home? You may want to read the last devotion in this book.

Something to think about.

- Do you listen to your conscience? If so, how does it sound to you?

- Do you believe faith in God can change people? Defend your answer.

- Why is faith important to God? What are your thoughts?

- Can Christians do everything by faith? Why or why not?

- Our sin was so ugly on Jesus during the crucifixion that God the Father could not look at his own Son during that time. Is this an accurate statement? Explain.

- Would you take the time to read the last devotion?

Your Relationship with Jesus

Think carefully about what is right, and stop sinning. For to your shame I say that some of you don't know God at all.
I Corinthians 15:34 NLT

Occasionally, someone will tell you to think. Use your brain, or don't waste your talent. Do you roll your eyes and want to say something when you hear those words?

Everything has a cause and effect, according to science. Those are just words in a book until there's a personal application. Then we get mad about something without finding out the cause. We dwell only on its undesirable impact.

If we thought more about the right words to choose before we spoke, we'd stay out of some hot water.

Thinking and doing right can be two different things. However, "think before you speak" can spare you some grief.

There's another thought about speaking too soon. "Stop sinning!" We commit more verbal sins than action sins. For example, at times, we assassinate the reputations of classmates. Sometimes, beyond repair or apology. But, once the words are out of our mouths, they're out. Never to return and impossible to cover up.

We can apologize, but the hurt doesn't go away. Not now, not tomorrow. Nor can an apology erase the emotional scars.

The devotional verse above doesn't stop with the first sentence. There is a continuation. There's one more issue, our relationship with God. Do you know Jesus as Savior? You can never develop your spiritual life without him. Knowing Jesus personally makes heaven your home. Salvation empowers the believer to think and live the way God desires. Jesus has a way of helping each believer live better every day. Really. He does.

Would you read the last devotion if there's a doubt about knowing Jesus as Savior?

Something to think about.

- How do you react when you hear unwanted suggestions?

- Have you read the advice of a parent in a magazine, and it made sense when it didn't before? Why?

- Have you ever said the right thing in the wrong way? Do the right words with an arrogant attitude help or hinder the gospel? Explain.

- Sometimes being quiet is better than speaking. Why?

- Reading the last devotion may change your eternity. Will you take the time to read it?

- Did the reading help you? How?

The Answer

*These things I have written to you who believe
in the name of the Son of God, so that you may know
that you have eternal life.*
I John 5:13 NASB

This devotion is for the questioner, the curious. Those who want to know and settle that gnawing in your soul. Is God real? Does he care about me? The real answer is yes! Emphatically yes.

A deliberate wrong is called a sin by the Bible. Everyone sins, but some have their sins forgiven, and others choose not to ask.

The Bible says the result of sin is physical death. So, death happens to everyone, but what happens afterward is eternally important to every individual.

The Bible is very plain. We all go into eternity. The question is, where? The Bible describes only two places. Heaven to be with Jesus (2 Corinthians 5:8) or the Lake of Fire (Revelation 20:15).

So, how do we know where we'll go?

Those who ask Jesus to forgive them of all their sins and come into their heart will experience salvation (Romans 10:9-13). However, for those who don't accept God's Son as Savior, the opposite is true (John 3:18). The last book of the New Testament describes the final judgment of those without Christ. Their ultimate eternal destination is the Lake of Fire (Revelation 20:11-15).

So, how does an individual ask Jesus into their heart? The answer is a prayer like the one below.

"Dear Lord Jesus, I know I'm a sinner. Without you in my heart, I'll die eventually and go to hell. "So, I'm asking you to forgive me of all my sins. Would you come into my heart and give me eternal life with you? Thank you, Jesus, for saving me from the Lake of Fire. In Jesus' name, I ask this. Amen."

What did you do? You asked Jesus to forgive you of all your sins and make heaven your eternal home. And God answered your prayer.

Sometime in the future, someone will try to confuse you about what you prayed. In your prayer, you asked God to give you eternal life. He did. And no one can take it from you. Jesus wants you to know you have eternal life (I John 5:13 ESV). Accepting Jesus is forever. (You may desire to read verses 13-15 to settle any existing doubts in your mind.)

The next step is to find a Bible-believing church and serve the Lord in it. Then, you'll soon realize that God has enriched your life forever.

Something to think about.

- Are you inquisitive? If so, in what areas? Write your short answer.

- What is your definition of sin? Do you think God would agree with you? Why or why not?

- Do you agree or disagree that there are only two eternal destinations? Defend your answer in a paragraph.

- Describe what it will be like to be with Jesus for eternity.

- Describe your understanding of the Lake of Fire (Revelation 20:11-15).

- How has knowing you will have eternal life helped you in your daily life?

Something to Think About

Eternity is in everybody's future. It doesn't make any difference whether you believe it or not. The question is, what are you going to do about it? You can read on and decide, or you can stop reading and go on with your life. But if you are serious about knowing your eternal destination—read on.

Curiosity has brought you here. The Bible says, "All Scripture is inspired by God and is useful to teach us what is true and to make us realize what is wrong in our lives" (2 Timothy 3:16). So, what does the Bible say about how to go to heaven?

There must be a realization something is missing in your life. Your conscience and the Bible agree, "No one is righteous—not even one" (Romans 3:10). Because we do not do right all the time, we choose to sin in the eyes of God. Once again, the Bible tells us our ill will eventually result in death. That happens to everybody. But what happens afterward is a choice we make here on this earth.

Our decision to accept, reject or ignore scripture is a personal decision. The Bible book of Romans is very plain in stating our status before God. However, this book also gives the remedy. Chapter ten of Romans, verses ten and eleven, states, "For it is by believing in your heart that you are made right with God, and it is by confessing with your mouth that you are saved. As the Scriptures tell us, 'Anyone who trusts in him will never be disgraced.'" Then verse thirteen adds, "Everyone who calls on the name of the LORD will be saved."

So how does a person ask Jesus into their heart? By sincerely praying a prayer like the following.

Dear Lord Jesus, I'm asking you to come into my heart and give me eternal life with you. Thank you for allowing me to spend eternity with you. In Jesus' name, I ask this.

This sincere prayer changes your eternal destination from hell to heaven. It also means you can now live a better life for Jesus (2 Corinthians 5:17).

Somewhere someone will try to confuse you about eternity. Once again, scripture has the answer. I John 5:13 states, "I have written this to you who believe in the name of the Son of God, so that you may know you have eternal life." God gave you eternal life with him; no one is powerful enough to take it from you!

Now find a Bible-practicing church and serve the Lord in it. When you do, you will grow in the Lord's knowledge. In addition, your regular attendance will help you learn how to live in a way that is pleasing to him.

The scripture in this section quotes the NLT.

Thank you for taking the DARE to START. The Lord will be with you to the finish line.

Milton Keynes UK
Ingram Content Group UK Ltd.
UKHW020642291123
433416UK00018B/1420